Contents

Abstract

Mexico's Troublesome Triangle: Poverty, Education, and Emigration. The issues of poverty, education, and emigration are intertwined in Mexico. Each issue directly affects the others with poverty being the main shared component. Further analysis indicates that these issues in turn affect the United States with illegal immigration at the forefront of these three issues. This paper researches these three components and discusses how they affect each other and in turn effect the economic development of southern Mexico. Furthermore, current changes in Mexico's education system are discussed and how these changes have affected poverty and illegal immigration with the changing economic situation in the United States. Finally, this paper recommends changes in the education of immigrant children and in the education of teachers who have immigrant students – both in the United States and in Mexico.

Introduction

Illegal immigration into the United States poses a credible threat to national security. The most contentious border is the one between the United States and Mexico. Issues of poverty, lack of education, and a need of job opportunities in Mexico have exacerbated this highly divisive matter. The United States could focus on other matters of national security instead of border control issues if it were to work with Mexico to alleviate issues in education. This in turn would stem the tide of poverty and increase job opportunities in Mexico, thus reducing illegal immigration.

While the Mexican government mandates compulsory basic education, ability of students to attend school varies throughout the country. This variation is mainly based on a family's financial situation and its location within Mexico – with the more impoverished families in the southern region. Hence, the education system in Mexico continues to need steadfast improvement and this situation affects issues of illegal immigration with the United States.

While Mexico has made strides recently in improving its education system, there remain problems that still need to be addressed. In discussing these issues, there are limitations to the scope of this thesis. Issues surrounding private/religious schools, technical schools, tertiary education, and differences in gender will not be broached. In addition, research was limited to more recent literature on this subject.

Critical Viewpoints and Counterarguments

On the other hand, critics might argue that the current education system is good enough – adequate money is being spent in Mexico on its education system. Currently, Mexico is spending 22 percent of public non-capital spending on education and this is the highest rate in the Organization for Economic Co-operation and Development (OECD).[1] OECD is an organization of 34 advanced and emerging countries dedicated to global development, which Mexico joined in 1994. In addition, this rate of educational spending in Mexico "amounts to 5.9 percent of the gross domestic product (GDP) per capita, above OECD's average of 5.6 percent."[2]

Furthermore, per Latin American standards, Mexico's school system is quite good and it has the second-best educated students in the region following Chile.[3] Currently, enrollment in primary schools is at an impressive 94 percent of children in Mexico.[4] Moreover, in Mexico's secondary level of education, the number of students has increased by more than two million since 1994 and the number of prepatory schools for students from 15 to 18 years of age has doubled in the more rural areas.[5]

Critics could also argue that this increase in educational spending and expansion in student attendance have thus lowered the level of Mexican emigration.[6] Figures show that illegal immigration to the United States dropped from 525,000 annually from 2000-2004 to

---

[1] "Education in Mexico, Schooling the Whole Family," *The Economist,* 12 May 2011, 1.
[2] Lucrecia Santibañez, Georges Vernez, and Paula Razquin, *Education in Mexico, Challenges and Opportunities*, Documented Briefing (Santa Monica, CA: RAND Corporation, 2005), vii.
[3] "Education in Mexico, Schooling the Whole Family," 1.
[4] Merilee S. Grindle, "Education Reform in Mexico," *ReVista, Harvard Review of Latin America,* Fall 2001, http://www.drclas harvard.edu/revista/articles/view/74 (accessed 10 October 2011).
[5] Ben Lamport, "Mexico's Improving Education and Declining Emigration," *Council on Hemispheric Affairs Blog*, 28 July 2011, http://cohaforum.org/2011/07/28/mexico%E2%80%99s-improving-education-and-declining-emigration/ (accessed 10 October 2011).
[6] Ibid, 2.

less than 100,000 in 2010.[7] Experts agree that this decrease in emigration can be directly attributed to increased education and employment opportunities at home, which only enforces the belief that the education system in Mexico is quite good.[8]

Mexican Educational Spending

While the counterarguments may indicate that Mexico's education system is in fact doing well, in reality the opposite is true. Although Mexico has increased it's spending on education, how the money is spent is the issue that unveils the poor performance. In comparison with other countries in the OECD, Mexico spends 80 percent of non-capital education spending on teachers' salaries compared to the OECD average of 64 percent.[9] Nonetheless, Mexico has made concerted attempts over the years to restructure, reorganize, and modernize its education system beginning in 1992 when the government decentralized the school system and transferred responsibility to the states.[10] However, "after all the changes in the last two decades, the Mexican education system still needs major modification and funding to modernize and improve services."[11]

While Mexico does spend an average amount of its GDP on education as compared to other countries in the OECD, this money goes toward teachers' salaries and not into improvements in the schools, curriculums, or infrastructure – exacerbating an already difficult situation.[12] To begin with, one of the main roadblocks to fundamental changes exists in the unfettered power of the teachers' union – the Sindicato Nacional de

---

[7] Damien Cave, "For Mexicans Looking North, a New Calculus Favors Home," *The New York Times*, 5 July 2011, http://www.nytimes.com/interactive/2011/07/06/world/americas/immigration.html (accessed 10 October 2011).
[8] Ibid, 2-3.
[9] "Education in Mexico, Schooling the Whole Family," 1.
[10] Luis A. Rosado, Marisa Hellawell, and Ezequiel Benedicto Zamora, *An Analysis of the Education Systems in Mexico and the United States from Pre-kinder to 12 Grade*, research article, 16 June 2011, 5.
[11] Ibid, 5.
[12] "Time to Wake Up," *The Economist*, 18 November 2006, 8.

Trabajadores de la Educación (SNTE) – arguably "the largest and probably most powerful union in all of Latin America."[13] While the Mexican government has continued to push for alterations and has enacted budget changes to improve schools, the union has continued to fight these changes. Currently, "nearly all of the money has gone on teachers' salaries," which further shows the powerful hold the union has on Mexico's education system.[14] To make matters worse, a 2008 audit of a single funding program showed that over 90,000 recipients' records contained irregularities and unbelievably "many of Mexico's teachers are imaginary or dead."[15] Furthermore, while the teachers' union should be pushing for improvements in schooling, infrastructure, and curriculums, it is instead much better at pursuing salary demands.[16] Consequently, given this strong hold the teachers' union has on Mexico's education system, it appears likely that major changes to the status quo are simply not going to happen anytime soon.[17]

The second area where there are inadequacies in Mexico's education spending can be found in the large disparity of spending between the northern and southern regions of the country. Even by Latin American standards, the inequality in Mexican education is large – individuals in the poorest fifth of the population have 3.5 years of schooling versus 11.6 years for individuals in the richest fifth.[18] In addition, even though education is compulsory, "there is still far from complete compliance. . . in some of the more rural areas."[19] While the North Atlantic Free Trade Agreement (NAFTA) has assisted in enriching northern Mexico with visible progress in infrastructure and wealth, southern Mexico continues to have

---

[13] Grindle, "Education Reform in Mexico," 1.
[14] "Time to Wake Up," 8.
[15] "Education in Mexico, Schooling the Whole Family," 1.
[16] "Time to Wake Up," 9.
[17] Ibid, 8.
[18] David McKenzie and Hillel Rapoport, *Migration and Education Inequality in Rural Mexico*, working paper (Buenos Aires, Argentina: Institute for the Integration of Latin America and the Caribbean, November 2006), 2.
[19] Ibid, 7.

widespread poverty and lack even the most basic infrastructure, worsening issues of adequate education.[20] Although the south is making strides in education advancements, quality continues to lag due to the disparity of federal funding dominating in the richer north.[21]

To be fair, the poverty and lack of basic infrastructure in the south make issues of education even more difficult. Because basic facilities or even roads are not available, having a school, let alone getting to school, can be very difficult. In addition, given how poverty affects a family, its members' focus shifts from education to the more basic necessities and children are forced to assist in filling rudimentary needs such as supplying food and water.[22] It is important to understand that the primary reason for children dropping out of school is the need to work, and given that poverty is more prominent in the south, the south suffers more from this situation.[23] To alleviate some of the issues of lack of infrastructure in the south, Mexico is using technology to improve rural schooling with digital textbooks and internet schooling – but in many rural southern towns, there is no internet connection.[24] Major challenges are still ahead for Mexico's education system and it needs to focus educational spending more on improvements in basic infrastructure and educational materials. In addition, Mexico must continue to work towards reducing the geographical inequalities between the northern urban and southern rural regions.[25]

A third area where educational spending in Mexico needs attention is in the area of educational evaluation and research. Lack of attention in this area directly affects efforts to

---

[20] "Time to Wake Up," 4.

[21] Ibid, 9.

[22] Chris Hawley, "Mexico's Objective: Better Education = Better Jobs," *USA Today*, 1 May 2008, http://www.usatoday.com/news/education/2008-04-30-mexicoschools_N htm (accessed 10 October 2011).

[23] "Education in Mexico, Schooling the Whole Family," 2.

[24] "Time to Wake Up," 9.

[25] Juan L. Ordaz-Díaz, "The Economic Returns to Education in Mexico: A Comparison Between Urban and Rural Areas," *Cepal Review*, December 2008, http://www.eclac.cl/publicaciones/xml/5/35765/RVI96OrdazDiaz.pdf (accessed 23 September 2011).

inform school improvements.[26] While the Ministry of Education does conduct research for

its own internal purposes, it does not make it publicly available, which limits further analysis

of the data collected.[27] In addition, spending on educational research and development was a

mere 0.4 percent of GDP whereas other countries such as the United States, Canada, and

Finland spent a minimum of 2 percent of GDP in this area.[28] On top of this, between 2000-

2006 there was a decrease in Mexico's GDP expenditure for the development of research and

technology.[29] The Centre for Educational Research and Innovation (CERI), a major division

of the OECD Directorate for Education, reviewed Mexico's educational research and

development program from 2003-2004. The evaluation found that while Mexico's education

system had recent developments, these developments were "not accompanied by an increase

in the capacity to produce research both for nurturing policy-makers and practitioners'

needs."[30]

Mexico's lack of research and evaluation in education is directly correlated with the

performance of its students in various standardized testing and reflects in its graduation rates.

Basically, educational spending in Mexico is not focused – areas such as curriculum

improvement, teacher training, classroom technology, and infrastructure improvements are

now clearly seen as impediments to students' abilities. This is especially obvious in the

results of OECD testing in 2007. OECD administers the Programme for International

Student Assessment (PISA) test every three years to assess attainment of knowledge and

---

[26] Santibañez, "Education in Mexico, Challenges and Opportunities," viii.
[27] Ibid, ix.
[28] Ordaz-Díaz, "The Economic Returns to Education in Mexico: A Comparison Between Urban and Rural Areas," 269.
[29] José G. Vargas-Hernández, "A Study of Education in Mexico, Issues and Challenges in the Economic, Political, and Social Trends." *International Journal of Education*, 2010 http://www.macrothink.org/journal/index.php/ije/article/view/529/370 (accessed 23 September 2011).
[30] Organization for Economic Co-operation and Development (OECD), *Policy Brief on Mexico: Education*, OECD Policy Note (Paris, France: Directorate for Education, September 2006), 7.

skills in students. Of the 30 countries that participated in the 2007 test, "Mexico came in last place in science, math and reading."[31] Furthermore, OECD ranks Mexico's education system at the bottom of its rankings.[32]

The effects on graduation rates are equally visible in the data. According to Mexico's National Institute of Statistics, Geography, and Information Processing, only 47 percent of students who begin vocational high school graduate and only 60 percent of students who begin college-prep high schools graduate.[33] In comparison, 75 percent of all high school students in the United States graduate.[34] Furthermore, these issues translate into students who lack basic skills and knowledge. For example, in the OECD countries, the majority of students have attained at least a minimum skill level in mathematical proficiency whereas the portion of Mexican students who have not attained this minimum skill level is 60 percent.[35] Expanding this issue further, in basic problem solving in assessing mathematical skills, only half of Mexico's students were able to solve simple problems compared to the OECD average of 22 percent.[36] Even when limiting discussion of Mexico's performance within the Latin American region, its students' performance is amongst the lowest.[37]

Effects of Poverty

In analyzing poverty in Mexico, there is an important underlying link between both poverty and a lack of education, and poverty and illegal immigration. The commonality between the two key aspects of this thesis and poverty creates important ties between the three issues. Even though school is available to just about every child, poverty continues to

---

[31] Hawley, "Mexico's Objective: Better Education = Better Jobs," 2.
[32] "Education in Mexico, Schooling the Whole Family," 1.
[33] Hawley, "Mexico's Objective: Better Education = Better Jobs," 2.
[34] Ibid.
[35] "Policy Brief on Mexico: Education," 4.
[36] Ibid, 5.
[37] Santibañez, "Education in Mexico, Challenges and Opportunities," ix.

limit educational opportunities in Mexico. As discussed earlier, there is a clear disparity of income between the northern and southern regions of Mexico and while "income inequality now is no greater than it was 20 years ago. . . regional differences are becoming increasingly marked" and NAFTA is helping to increase the regional education gap.[38] This education gap between urban and rural areas has expanded to a difference of approximately 10 years of education per student and justifies a greater push to accelerate improvements in education in the rural countryside.[39] Furthermore, official figures show that in Mexico, half of the population lives in some degree of poverty, while it increases to 75 percent in the south.[40]

This level of poverty in the south of Mexico directly affects education in the region. Since federal spending in Mexico is skewed toward the north and its existing infrastructure, the south continues to suffer in the quality of its schooling and in equality of opportunity.[41] Research has shown that within a population, levels of education are directly related to economic development.[42] In addition, education leads to further development of various skills and capabilities, which directly leads to higher earnings.[43] Furthermore, an increase in labor productivity affects rural earnings and poverty reduction, thus increasing the population's well being.[44]

Multiple studies have shown that there is an inverse correlation between poverty and education.[45] When combining this correlation with the fact that the education for the rural population is shorter in length and to a lower standard than in urban areas, it is easy to see

---

[38] "Time to Wake Up," 7.
[39] Ordaz-Díaz, "The Economic Returns to Education in Mexico: A Comparison Between Urban and Rural Areas," 267.
[40] "Time to Wake Up," 7.
[41] Ibid, 8.
[42] Ordaz-Díaz, "The Economic Returns to Education in Mexico: A Comparison Between Urban and Rural Areas," 266.
[43] Ibid.
[44] Ibid, 267.
[45] Ibid, 268.

where the Mexican government needs to focus its educational spending.[46] It has been shown that "education is the most effective way for people living in poverty to improve their economic status, and that allocating more resources to education could reduce economic inequality within a country."[47]

This lack of education in conjunction with poverty is a self-perpetuating phenomenon. However, Mexico is trying to help impoverished families break this cycle of poverty and improve these families' lifestyle enough to allow for more opportunities for the children in these families. While there is still a long way to go, Mexico's improvements in its education system are beginning to somewhat alleviate this cycle of poverty and its subsequent effects on illegal immigration. One of the programs that has been very successful in this endeavor is the conditional cash transfer (CCT) program called Opportunidades (formerly known as Progresa). CCTs are so successful that over 30 countries worldwide now use this type of program for the reason that "increasing human capital investments in children is considered to be among the most effective ways of encouraging growth and of alleviating poverty in developing countries."[48]

Opportunidades was introduced in Mexico in 1997 and currently assists over five million families throughout the country at a cost of $2 billion a year.[49] A greater portion of rural families, some 40 percent, are participating in the program, which in turn is helping to alleviate some of the severe poverty in the predominantly rural southern half of Mexico.[50] The purpose of the program is not to stop poverty, but to break the cycle and stop poverty in

---

[46] Ordaz-Díaz, "The Economic Returns to Education in Mexico: A Comparison Between Urban and Rural Areas," 279.

[47] Ibid.

[48] Jere Behrman, Piyali Sengupta, and Petra Todd, *Progressing Through Progresa: An Impact Assessment of a School Subsidy Experiment in Mexico,*" IFPRI PROGRESA Evaluation Project, 1.

[49] "Time to Wake Up," 7.

[50] Behrman, "Progressing Through Progresa: An Impact Assessment of a School Subsidy Experiment in Mexico" 1.

the next generation by expediting the transition of the labor force to one that has completed

secondary school.[51]

Opportunidades works by alleviating the opportunity cost of children in the family

attending school instead of working, and given that older children are more likely to work at

home or outside the home, the stipend increases as the child ages.[52] These stipends are also

contingent on regular preventative health checks.[53] Opportunidades recognizes that "poverty

is itself one reason why children drop out of school early."[54] The program has been very

successful and

> participation in the program is associated with higher enrollment rates, less grade
> repetition and better grade progression, lower dropout rates, and higher school reentry
> rates among dropouts. Particularly notable are the impacts on reducing dropout rates
> during the transition from primary to secondary school.[55]

Opportunidades has alleviated the pressure on impoverished families to require their children

to work instead of attending school and this in turn is leading to a new generation of better

educated children in Mexico.

Illegal Immigration

Issues of immigration, both legal and illegal, continue to be a divisive issue in both

the United States and Mexico. Given the geographic proximity of the two countries, this is

not an issue that is ever going away soon. Illegal immigration has been an issue for decades

now and while the focus has been predominantly on various political and economic aspects,

educational aspects of immigration are now becoming more prominent.[56] As previously

---

[51] "Time to Wake Up," 7.
[52] Behrman, "Progressing Through Progresa: An Impact Assessment of a School Subsidy Experiment in Mexico" 1.
[53] Ibid, 10.
[54] "Time to Wake Up," 7.
[55] Behrman, "Progressing Through Progresa: An Impact Assessment of a School Subsidy Experiment in Mexico" 22.
[56] Lonnie Rowell, Yara Amparo Lopez Lopez, Basthi Maribel King Ristori, Maria Mercedes

discussed, there is an undeniable tie among poverty, lack of education, and illegal immigration.

Every year, approximately 500,000 Mexicans cross into the United States in search of jobs and a better life.[57] These immigrants, both legal and illegal, tend to send money back to their families in Mexico. These remittances account for over $24 billion, more than foreign direct investment by a third.[58] The ability of these immigrants to send money back home is directly related to the pay they are able to get in the United States as compared to back home. If Mexico is to stem this tide of emigration, it has to take more active steps to reduce poverty and raise living standards in order to make remaining at home more attractive to young people.[59] In order to try and slow emigration to the United States, Mexico is currently working on new ways to modernize and create better paying jobs.[60]

Once again, the best way to reduce poverty and increase job opportunities is to increase education and while Mexico's education system has made great strides, it still has a long way to go in relation to other countries. But in relation to it's own previous educational attainments, Mexico has done quite well.[61] This is seen most clearly in the increased propensity for Mexican citizens to remain in the country in search of employment, which in turn has helped lower the rate of illegal immigration into the United States in recent years.[62]

In addition to educational changes, economic changes have also affected illegal immigration rates. Many businesses in Mexico have either been created or expanded with

Veyna Figueroa, Eva Mejia, Elizabeth Schlicher, Angel Chavarin, Briana Colorado, and Lea Garza, *Education and Migration – Mexico-United States: Opportunities for Binational Collaboration*, Border Brief (San Diego, CA: USD Trans-Border Institute, 9 August 2010), 1.
[57] "Time to Wake Up," 4.
[58] Ibid, 7.
[59] "Time to Wake Up," 11.
[60] Hawley, "Mexico's Objective: Better Education = Better Jobs," 1.
[61] Lamport, "Mexico's Improving Education and Declining Emigration," 1.
[62] Ibid.

these economic changes.[63] Furthermore, wages in Mexico have risen and the recession has

cut the wage disparity even further between the United States and Mexico, making it more

lucrative for an educated Mexican to seek employment within Mexico.[64] Moreover, family

income has risen by over 45 percent since 2000 in addition to equal gains in per capita

GDP.[65] Likewise, improvements have also occurred in the infrastructure of rural areas –

improvements such as electricity and running water.[66] These tangible increases in quality of

life, in addition to the increased employment prospects, have made it much easier for citizens

to choose to remain in the country.

Although the factors of education and improved economic conditions are two of the

prevalent factors in the reduction of illegal immigration, they are not the only factors. One of

the other factors affecting immigration rates is the current danger and expense involved in

crossing the border illegally due to the activities of drug cartels.[67] Another factor is the

shrinking size of Mexican families – down from an average 6.8 children in 1970 to about two

children currently.[68] An additional factor that stemmed illegal immigration is the fact that

life as an illegal immigrant in the United States became increasingly difficult with tougher

laws and increased deportation.[69] On the other hand, through changes in the United States'

immigration policy, legal immigration became easier and this also decreased illegal

immigration.[70]

---

[63] Cave, "For Mexicans Looking North, a New Calculus Favors Home," 3.
[64] Ibid.
[65] Ibid, 2.
[66] Ibid, 3.
[67] Ibid, 2.
[68] Ibid.
[69] Ibid, 4.
[70] Ibid.

However, numerous studies show that the strongest factor in the sharp decline in illegal immigration stems from Mexico's expanding education system.[71] While this decrease is a positive step in the divisive issue of immigration, there is no guarantee that this trend is permanent. When the economy in the United States recovers and is once again offering wages substantially higher than wages in Mexico, it will be interesting to see if the level of education once again rises to challenge and stem the tide of illegal immigrants and make working in Mexico just as attractive or if the issue of illegal immigration will return to previous levels seen years ago. Only through sustained coordination and cooperation can Mexico and the United States continue to work on common issues such as immigration and education.

Conclusions and Recommendations

Geography dictates that the relationship between the United States and Mexico will always remain vital to each country's interests, most importantly in the economic, diplomatic, and national security realms. As such, cooperation between the two countries concerning various shared issues will be paramount. Education is one such issue - and specifically how a lack of education ties directly to poverty and illegal immigration between Mexico and the United States. One aspect of education that can be improved is the education of immigrant children from both countries.

When children transfer between schools in their own country, they usually take with them a transcript with descriptions of the classes or proficiency levels that they have achieved. This allows for teachers and administrators in the new school system to place the

---

[71] Lamport, "Mexico's Improving Education and Declining Emigration," 2.

child in the appropriate grade level or class of instruction. However, when a child transfers between schools in two different countries, numerous problems can become evident.

Foremost in discussing these problems is the issue of immigrant children travelling between the United States and Mexico, or visa versa, and how the lack of a relevant transcript is detrimental to a child continuing in their education after a move between these countries. For example, when a child returns to Mexico after spending time in the school system of the United States, they "do so without academic records from their time in the U.S. educational system, thus making it difficult to certify credits for educational purposes."[72] This can lead to these students being placed in the new schools as auditors and therefore not eligible to receive credit for their schoolwork.[73] However, sometimes these students are instead given diagnostic tests to attempt to place them in the correct level. Yet these tests often cover knowledge that is outside the realm of subjects taught in the United States and thus these students do not perform well on these tests and are subsequently not placed in the appropriate academic class level.[74]

The remedy for this situation is a standardized transcript for students traveling in either direction between Mexico and the United States. Currently, there is no such program in place. However, while the curriculum may differ between the two countries, a clear documentation of classes taken and standardized test scores achieved could alleviate this issue and allow for these transfer students to be placed appropriately when they move. This type of improvement in the tracking of immigrant students' progress is important for both countries, as education is the primary factor affecting poverty. In addition, given the large number of immigrant children from Mexico living in the United States, legally or illegally,

---

[72] Rowell, "Education and Migration – Mexico-United States," 3.
[73] Ibid.
[74] Ibid.

14

and the large number of immigrant children returning to Mexico in recent years, this is a situation that neither country can afford to ignore. It is only through collaboration and cooperation that this situation with immigrant transfer students can be vastly improved – to the benefit of both countries and their economies.

The second issue surrounds the performance of immigrant children in school once they have transferred to another country. There are various factors that a child may be dealing with when they move – and it can be especially disorienting when crossing between countries. Issues such as trauma, grief, loneliness, and isolation can affect how well a student integrates into their new school.[75] Furthermore, "what is clear is that students emigrating from Mexico and entering mainstream U.S. schools face numerous hardships and stressors that serve as barriers to their academic and social success in schools."[76] In addition, "students from the U.S. entering schools in Mexico face many obstacles, difficulties, and challenges that are sometimes impossible to overcome, these students often decide to abandon their studies and enter the workforce or participate in anti-social behavior, such as drug abuse, graffiti, vandalism, and prostitution, among others."[77]

The solution to this problem is professional development for teachers and school administrators to become more aware of the distinct issues surrounding children of immigrant families.[78] This professional development needs to include addressing teachers' attitudes, as their attitudes towards these children are paramount in establishing trust and security, as well as emotional support, for these children during this transitory time while

---

[75] Rowell, "Education and Migration – Mexico-United States," 4.
[76] Ibid, 2.
[77] Ibid, 3.
[78] Ibid, 4.

settling into a new school.[79] In addition, "teachers need to facilitate students' adaptation to

their new environment."[80] This is best accomplished by integrating the cultural backgrounds

of these immigrant children into their lessons in class as "students need to be connected to

their cultural backgrounds" and this in turn helps these students succeed.[81]

Professional development for teachers also should include a basic knowledge and

understanding of the school system in the other country. For example, teachers in the United

States should know and understand that students in Mexico are "accustomed to seeing and

producing art" and if these teachers use this focus on art with immigrant students, it may help

in engaging these students.[82] In addition, teachers should be aware that students from

Mexico are accustomed to a less rigid daily time schedule, their school day is much shorter,

classrooms are much more informal, and there is more frequent group work.[83]

In facilitating the adjustment of immigrant students to their new country and the

environment in school, these teachers are enhancing the chances that these students will

continue in their education and graduate – instead of quitting school because of an inability

to adapt. Consequently, a more educated individual is more likely to become a productive

member of society, maintain a good job, and add to the economic prosperity of the country.

This prosperity enhances a country's stability and encourages economic growth and advances

in infrastructure. Basically, having better-educated students is equally advantageous to both

the United States and Mexico. In addition, with better educated students on both sides of the

---

[79] Rowell, "Education and Migration – Mexico-United States," 4.

[80] Ali Borjian and Amado M. Padilla, "Voices from Mexico: How American Teachers can Meet the Needs of Immigrant Students," *The Urban Review* 42, no. 4 (16 September 2009): 324.

[81] Ibid, 322.

[82] James H. McLaughlin, *Schooling in Mexico: A Brief Guide for U.S. Educators*, Information Analysis (Charleston, WV: ERIC Clearinghouse on Rural Education and Small Schools, December 2002), 4.

[83] Ibid.

shared border, the United States will not have as many illegal immigrants crossing the border and affecting aspects of National Security.

Final Remarks

Issues surrounding poverty, education, and illegal immigration in Mexico also affect the United States. Given that Mexico is one of only two countries that adjoin the United States, the relationship between the two countries will always be important. As such, when these issues of education and illegal immigration spill over from Mexico into the United States, there is now a commonality to the problem that only coordination, cooperation, and a basic understanding of the overarching situation in the other country that will help in resolving these matters. Furthermore, given the importance of the relationship and the degree to which each country is tied to the other, this combining of efforts is not only important, it is vital. By working in unison to address these problems, both countries will benefit and so will their citizens.

BIBLIOGRAPHY

Behrman, Jere, Piyali Sengupta, and Petra Todd. *Progressing Through Progresa: An Impact Assessment of a School Subsidy Experiment in Mexico.* IFPRI PROGRESA Evaluation Project. June 2002. http://pws.iadb.org/res/publications/pubfiles/pubS-221.pdf (accessed 23 September 2011).

Borjian, Ali, and Amado M. Padilla, "Voices from Mexico: How American Teachers can Meet the Needs of Mexican Immigrant Students." *The Urban Review* 42, no. 4 (16 September 2009): 316-328.

Cave, Damien. "For Mexicans Looking North, a New Calculus Favors Home," *The New York Times*, 6 July 2011. http://www.nytimes.com/interactive/2011/07/06/world/americas/immigration.html (accessed 10 October 2011)

Grindle, Merilee S. "Education Reform in Mexico." *ReVista, Harvard Review of Latin America*, Fall 2001. http://www.drclas.harvard.edu/revista/articles/view/74 (accessed 10 October 2011).

Hawley, Chris. "Mexico's objective: Better Education = Better Jobs," *USA Today*, 1 May 2008. http://www.usatoday.com/news/education/2008-04-30-mexicoschools_N.htm (accessed 10 October 2011).

Jensen, Bryant T., "Culture and Practice of Mexican Primary Schooling: Implications for Improving Policy and Practice in the U.S." *Current Issues in Education*, October 2005. http://cie.asu.edu/volume8/number24/ (accessed 17 October 2011).

Lamport, Ben. "Mexico's Improving Education and Declining Emigration," *Council on Hemispheric Affairs Blog*. 28 July 2011. http://cohaforum.org/2011/07/28/mexico%E2%80%99s-improving-education-and-declining-emigration/ (accessed 10 October 2011).

McKenzie, David and Hillel Rapoport. *Migration and Education Inequality in Rural Mexico*. Working Paper. Buenos Aires, Argentina: Institute for the Integration of Latin America and the Caribbean, November 2006. http://www.iadb.org/intal/aplicaciones/uploads/publicaciones/i_INTALITD_WP_23_2006_McKenzie_Rapoport.pdf (accessed 10 October 2011).

McLaughlin, James H. *Schooling in Mexico: A Brief Guide for U.S. Educators*. Information Analysis. Charleston, WV: ERIC Clearinghouse on Rural Education and Small Schools, December 2002.

Olavarrieta, Concepcion. "Reversing the Mexican 'Brain Drain.'" *The Futurist*, May/June 2011.

http://findarticles.com/p/articles/mi_go2133/is_201105/ai_n57625385/?tag=content;c ol1 (accessed 17 October 2011).

Ordaz-Díaz, Juan L. "The Economic Returns to Education in Mexico: A Comparison Between Urban and Rural Areas." *Cepal Review,* December 2008. http://www.eclac.cl/publicaciones/xml/5/35765/RVI96OrdazDiaz.pdf (accessed 23 September 2011).

Organization for Economic Co-operation and Development (OECD). *Policy Brief on Mexico: Education.* OECD Policy Note. Paris, France: Directorate for Education, September 2006. http://www.foropoliticaspublicas.org.mx/docs/Educacion.pdf (accessed 23 September 2011).

Rosado, Luis A., Marisa Hellawell, and Ezequiel Benedicto Zamora, *An Analysis of the Education Systems in Mexico and the United States from Pre-kinder to 12 Grade.* Research article. 16 June 2011. In Education Resources Information Center, ERIC #ED520900.

Rowell, Lonnie, Yara Amparo Lopez Lopez, Basthi Maribel King Ristori, Maria Mercedes Veyna Figueroa, Eva Mejia, Elizabeth Schlicher, Angel Chavarin, Briana Colorado, and Lea Garza, *Education and Migration – Mexico-United States: Opportunities for Binational Collaboration.* Border Brief. University of San Diego Trans-Border Institute, 9 August 2010. http://catcher.sandiego.edu/items/peacestudies/Microsoft%20Word%20- %20BorderBrief_9__CP_aug13_10.pdf (accessed 23 September 2011).

Santibañez, Lucrecia, Georges Vernez, and Paula Razquin. *Education in Mexico – Challenges and Opportunities.* Documented Briefing. Santa Monica, CA: Rand Corporation, 2005. http://www.rand.org/pubs/documented_briefings/2005/RAND_DB480.sum.pdf (accessed 31 August 2011).

Sawyer, Adam, "In Mexico, Mother's Education and Remittances Matter in School Outcomes." Migration Policy Institute, 29 March 2010. http://www.migrationinformation.org/Feature/display.cfm?ID=775 (accessed 10 October 2011).

The Economist, "Education in Mexico, Schooling the Whole Family." 12 May 2011. http://www.economist.com/node/18682699 (accessed 10 October 2011).

The Economist, "Time to Wake Up – A Survey of Mexico." 18 November 2006, 3-16.

Vargas-Hernández, José G., "A Study of Education in Mexico, Issues and Challenges in the Economic, Political, and Social Trends." *International Journal of Education*, 2010 Vol. 2, No. 2. http://www.macrothink.org/journal/index.php/ije/article/view/529/370 (accessed 23 September 2011).